Applied Psychology

Volume 6

PSYCHIC ENERGY

Being the Sixth of a Series of Twelve Volumes on the Applications of Psychology to the Problems of Personal and Business Efficiency

BY

WARREN HILTON, A.B., L.L.B.

FOUNDER OF THE SOCIETY OF APPLIED PSYCHOLOGY

ISSUED UNDER THE AUSPICES OF

THE LITERARY DIGEST

FOR

The Society of Applied Psychology

NEW YORK AND LONDON

1920

**Republished from the public domain
by**

Creative English Publishing

www.Creative-English-Institute.com

Under Classic Reads

August 2013

**ISBN-13:
978-1492218326**

**ISBN-10:
1492218324**

CONTENTS

Chapter I
Mental Second Wind
PAGE 11

STICKING TO THE JOB

THE LAGGING BRAIN

RESERVE SUPPLIES OF POWER

"BLUE" MONDAYS

HOW TO STRIKE ONE'S STRIDE

THE SPUR OF DESIRE

HOW TO RELEASE STORED-UP
ENERGIES

THE LAWYER WHO "OVERWORKS"

EXCITEMENT AND THE HERO

ENDURING POWER OF MIND

Chapter II
RESERVES OF POWER
PAGE 23

MAN'S POTENTIAL AND KINETIC ENERGIES

HOLDING THE TOP PACE

GENIUS AND THE MASTER MAN

MENTAL EFFECTS OF CITY LIFE

NEW-FOUND ENERGIES EXPLAINED

QUICKENED MENTALITY

FAST LIVING AND LONG LIVING

PROFESSOR PATRICK'S EXPERIMENTS

RATIO BETWEEN REPAIR AND DEMAND

PYGMIES AND GIANTS

TRANSFORMING INERTNESS INTO ALERTNESS

HOW THE MIND ACCUMULATES ENERGY

THE THRESHOLD OF INHIBITION

HIDDEN STRENGTH

GIVING A MAN SCOPE

Chapter III
THE INITIATIVE ENERGY OF SUCCESS
PAGE 41

SOURCES OF PERSISTENCE

IMPORTANCE OF THE MENTAL SETTING

IDEAS ALL MEN RESPOND TO

HOW TO EXALT THE PERSONALITY

"GOOD STARTERS" AND "STRONG FINISHERS"

STEPS IN SELF-DEVELOPMENT

SAVING A THOUSAND A YEAR

LOOKING FOR A "SOFT SNAP"

DRAWING POWER FROM ON HIGH

THE MAN WHO LASTS

Chapter IV
HOW TO AVOID WASTES THAT DRAIN THE ENERGY OF SUCCESS
PAGE 53

SPEEDING THE BULLET WITHOUT AIMING

WHY MOST MEN FAIL

THE SUCCESSFUL PROMOTER

THE HUMAN DYNAMO

COOL BRAINS AND HOT BOXES

MARVELOUS INCREASED EFFICIENCY HANDLING "PIG"

"OVERLOADED" HUMAN ENGINES

SCIENTIFIC MANAGEMENT OF SELF

PHYSIOLOGICAL CAUSES OF WASTE

TESTS FOR SENSORY DEFECTS

MENTAL FRICTION AND INNER WHIRLWINDS

PROMINENT TRAITS OF GREAT ACHIEVERS

WHY A MAN BREAKS DOWN

HOW TO ECONOMIZE EFFORT

HOW YOUR MENTAL CAPITAL IS DISSIPATED

CONQUERING INDECISION

WHY "CHRISTIAN SCIENCE" WORKS

HOW TO RELEASE PENT-UP POWER

PROPER RATIO BETWEEN WORK AND REST

DETERMINING YOUR NORM OF EFFICIENCY

Chapter V
THE SECRET OF MENTAL EFFICIENCY
PAGE 79

WHERE ENERGY IS STORED

BODILY EFFECTS OF IDEAS

IMPULSES AND INHIBITIONS

TRAINING FOR MENTAL "TEAM-WORK"

RUST AND THE "DAILY GRIND"

IDEAS THAT HARMONIZE

FIVE RULES FOR CONSERVING ENERGY

BUSINESS LUCK AND "BLUE-SKY" THEORIES

DEVICES FOR COMMERCIAL EFFICIENCY

Chapter I

MENTAL SECOND WIND

Sticking to the Job

Are you an unusually persevering and persistent person? Or, like most of us, do you sometimes find it difficult to stick to the job until it is done? What is your usual experience in this respect?

Is it not this, that you work steadily along until of a sudden you become conscious of a feeling of weariness, crying "Enough!" for the time being, and that you then yield to the impulse to stop?

The Lagging Brain

Assuming that this is what generally happens, does this feeling of fatigue, this impulse to rest, mean that your mental energy is exhausted?

Suppose that by a determined effort of the will you force your lagging brain to take up the thread of work. There will invariably come a new supply of energy, a "second wind," enabling you to forge ahead with a freshness and vigor that is surprising after the previous lassitude.

Nor is this all. The same process may be repeated a second time and a third time, each new effort of the will being followed by a renewal of energy.

Reserve Supplies of Power

Many a man will tell you that he does his best work in the wee watches of the morning, after tedious hours of persevering but fruitless effort. Instead of being exhausted by its long hours of persistent endeavor, the mind seems now to rise to the acme of its power, to achieve its supreme accomplishments. Difficulties melt into thin air, profound problems find easy solution. Flights of genius manifest themselves. Yet long before midnight such a one had perhaps felt himself yield to fatigue and had tied a wet towel around his head or had taken stimulants to keep himself awake.

The existence of this reserve supply of energy is manifested in physical as well as mental effort.

Men who work with their heads and men who work with their hands, scholars and Marathon runners, must alike testify to the existence of reserve supplies of power not ordinarily drawn upon.

"Blue" Mondays

If we do not always or habitually utilize this reserve power, it is simply because we have accustomed ourselves to yield at once to the first strong feeling of fatigue.

Evidence of this same fact appears in our feelings on different days. How often does a man get up from his breakfast-table after a long night's rest, when he should be feeling fresh and invigorated, and say to himself, "I don't feel like working today." And it may take him until afternoon to get into his workaday stride, if, indeed, he reaches it at all.

How to Strike One's Stride

You cannot yourself be immune from the feeling on certain days that you are not at your best. Somehow or other, your wits seem befogged. You hesitate to undertake important interviews. Your interest lags. And though crises arise in your business, you feel weighted down and unable to meet them with that shrewd discernment and decisiveness of action of which you know yourself capable.

But you realize, in your inmost self, that if you continue to exert the will and persistently hold yourself to the business in hand, sooner or later you will warm to the work, enthusiasm will come, the clouds will be dispelled, the husks will fly. Yet you have had no rest; on the contrary, you have, by continued conscious effort, consumed more and more of your vital energy.

The Spur of Desire

Obviously it was not rest that you needed.

What you required was the impulse of some strong desire that should carry you over the threshold of that first inertia into the wide field of reserve energy so rarely called upon and so rich in power.

Under the lashings of necessity, or the spur of love or ambition, men accomplish feats of mental and physical endurance of which they would have supposed themselves incapable. Here is what a certain lawyer says of his early struggles:

How to Release Stored-Up Energies

"When I was twenty-three years old, married, and with a family to support, I entered the law course of a great university. Of the many students in my class, seven, including me, were making a living while studying law.

"By special arrangement, I was relieved from attendance at lectures and simply required to pass examinations on the various subjects, and was thus enabled to retain my place as principal of a large public school. During the third and last year of my law course, I was principal of a public day school of two thousand children and an alternate night school with an enrolment of seven hundred and fifty, and I worked at the law three nights in the week and all day Sunday.

The Lawyer Who "Overworks"

"After eight months of this, the final examinations came around. They consumed a full week—from nine in the morning until five or six at night. I had no opportunity for review, so I rented a room near the law school to save the time going and coming and reviewed each night the subjects of examination for the following day.

"I did not sleep more than two hours any night in that week. On Thursday, while bolting a bit of luncheon, a fishbone stuck in my throat. Fearful of losing the result of my year's effort, I returned to my work, suffering much pain, and kept at it until Saturday night, when the examinations were concluded. The next day the surgeon who removed the fishbone said there was no reason why I should not have had 'a bad case of gangrene.'

"When I look back on that year's work I don't see how I stood it. I don't see how I kept myself at it, day in, day out, month after month without rest, recreation or relief. I am sure I could never go through it again, even if I had the courage to undertake it.

"I ranked second in a class of one hundred and eighty in my law examinations, won the second prize for the best graduating thesis, received a complimentary vote for class orator ship, and much to my surprise was soon after offered an assistant super-intendency of the public schools by the school board, who knew nothing of my studies and thought my work as a teacher worthy of promotion.

"It was not only the hardest year's work but the best year's work I ever did. It exemplifies my invariable experience that the more we want to do the more we can do and the better we can do it."

Excitement and the Hero

The following is an extract from a letter quoted by Professor James as written by Colonel Baird-Smith after the siege of Delhi in 1857, to the success of which he largely contributed:

"My poor wife had some reason to think that war and disease, between them, had left very little of a husband to take under nursing when she got him again. An attack of scurvy had filled my mouth with sores, shaken every joint in my body and covered me all over with scars and livid spots, so that I was unlovely to look upon. A smart knock on the ankle joint from the splinter of a shell that burst in my face, in itself a mere bagatelle of a wound, had been of necessity neglected under the pressing and insistent calls upon me, and had grown worse and worse until the whole foot below the ankle became a black mass and seemed to threaten mortification. I insisted, however, on being allowed to use it until the place was taken, mortification or no; and though the pain was sometimes horrible I carried my point and kept up to the last.

"On the day after the assault I had an unlucky fall on some bad ground, and it was an open question for a day or two whether I hadn't broken my arm at the elbow. Fortunately it turned out to be only a severe sprain, but I am still conscious of the wrench it gave me. To crown the whole pleasant catalogue, I was worn to a shadow by a constant diarrhea and consumed as much opium as would have done credit to my father-in-law (Thomas De Quincey).

"However, thank God, I have a good share of Tapleyism in me and come out strong under difficulties. I think I may confidently say that no man ever saw me out of heart or ever heard a complaining word from me even when our prospects were gloomiest. We were sadly crippled by cholera, and it was almost appalling to me to find that out of twenty-seven officers I could only muster fifteen for the operations of the attack. However, it was done,—and after it was done came the collapse.

Enduring Power of Mind

"Don't be horrified when I tell you that for the whole of the actual siege, and in truth for some little time before, I almost lived on brandy. Appetite for food I had none, but I forced myself to eat just sufficient to sustain life, and I had an incessant craving for brandy, as the strongest stimulant I could get. Strange to say, I was quite unconscious of its affecting me in the slightest degree.

"The excitement of the work was so great that no lesser one seemed to have any chance against it, and I certainly never found my intellect clearer or my nerves stronger in my life."

Such is the profound resourcefulness and enduring power of the human mind.

Chapter II

RESERVES OF POWER

Man's Potential and Kinetic Energies

Stored-up energy not in use has been given a name by scientific men. They call it potential energy. In this way it is distinguished from kinetic or circulating energy by which is meant energy that is at work. For example, a ton of coal in the bin contains a certain amount of potential energy, which is capable of being converted into kinetic energy by combustion.

Holding the Top Pace

You have a vast amount of potential energy over and above what you actually use. You have formed the habit of giving up trying a thing as soon as you have spent the usual amount of effort on it, and this without regard to whether or not you have accomplished anything.

While we all have the power of sustained mental activity, not one in ten thousand of us holds to the top pace.

Worse still, even such mental energy as we do consume is dispersed and scattered over a multitude of trivial interests instead of being focused upon someone possessing aim.

We intend to show you how you can lose yourself in your work with an absorbing passion and how you can at any time make special requisition upon your hidden stores of potential energy and draw new supplies of power that will sweep you on to your goal.

Genius and the Master Man

More than anything else, it is the ability to do this that lifts the great men of the race above the common run of mortals.

It is this that distinguishes genius from mediocrity. The master man transforms his vast stores of reserve or potential energy into circulating or kinetic energy. His work glows with living fire.

Yet, for every such man there are a multitude of others, equally gifted in some respect, but wanting that mysterious "Open Sesame" which would discover their hidden mental riches, arouse them from their accustomed inferiority to their best selves, and transform potentiality into accomplishment. So it comes about that most of us are gems that shine but to illumine the "dark unfathomed caves of ocean," flowers born to "blush unseen."

Mental Effect of City Life

Take an illustration of the way in which this reserve or potential energy is transformed into circulating or kinetic energy. Suppose that you are a countryman and come to live in a large city. The speed with which we do things, our habits of quick decision, the whirlwind of activities of the busy man in town, appal you. You cannot see how we live through it. A day in the business district fills you with terror. The tumult and danger make it seem "like a permanent earthquake."

But settle down to work here. And in a year you will have "caught the pulse beat," you will "vibrate to the city's rhythm," and if you only "make good" in your work, you will enjoy the strain and hurry, you will keep pace with the best of us, and you will get more out of yourself in a day in the city than you ever did in a week on the farm.

This change in degree of mental activity does not necessarily mean that you are making more of a success of life.

Your activities may be ill-directed. Your new-found powers may be misspent and dissipated.

But you are mentally more alert. Your mental forces have been stimulated by the stirring environment.

New-Found Energies Explained

And, mark this particularly, a number of mental pictures will pass across the screen of your consciousness today in the same time that one mental image formerly required.

Now, you have learned that with every idea catalogued in memory, there is wrapped up and stowed away an associated "feeling tone" and an associated impulse to some particular muscular action.

Assuming this, you must at once see that here is an explanation of your new-found energy.

Your quickened step, your new-found decisiveness of action, your more observant eye, your clear-cut speech instead of the former drawling utterance, your livelier manner, your freshened enthusiasm and enjoyment of life—all of these are but manifestations of a quickened intelligence.

Quickened Mentality

They are the working out through the motor paths of mental impulses to muscular action.

And these impulses to muscular action come thronging into consciousness because the livelier environment brings about a more rapid reproduction of memory pictures.

And here comes a particularly striking fact. One would naturally suppose that the more energy a man consumed, and the faster he lived, the more quickly his vitality would be exhausted and the shorter his life would be.

As a matter of fact, by the divine beneficence of Providence, your organism is so ordered as to adapt itself within certain wide limits to the demands made upon it.

Fast Living and Long Living

You may call into play all the stored-up resources of your being and still not stake everything upon a single throw. For the supply of mental energy is as inexhaustible as the reservoir of all past experience, while the supply of physical energy involved in brain and nerve activity is, like the immortal liver of Prometheus, renewed as fast as depleted.

Two sets of facts that have been established by elaborate scientific experiment will convince you of the truth of these propositions.

Professor Patrick's Experiments

Professor Patrick, of the State University of Iowa, conducted some of these experiments. He caused three young men to remain awake for four successive days and nights. They were then allowed to go to sleep, the purpose of the experiment being to determine just how much time Nature required to recuperate from the long vigil. They were allowed to sleep themselves out, and all woke up thoroughly rested. Yet the one who slept the longest slept only one-third longer than his customary night's sleep.

You have doubtless had the same experience yourself many times. It all goes to show that if we are awake four times as long as usual, we do not make up for it by sleeping four times as long, but four times as soundly, as customary. The hard-working mechanic requires no more hours of sleep than the corner loafer, the active man of affairs no more than the dawdler.

Ratio Between Repair and Demand

The time of tissue repair is about the same with all men under all conditions. It is the rate of repair that varies with the demand that has been put upon the body.

Again, look at the same subject from the standpoint of food supply. On what you now eat and drink you have a certain average weight. Eat, digest and assimilate a larger quantity of food and your weight will increase. This increase will be greatest at the start and will gradually slow up until you shall have reached the point beyond which you can gain no more. Given the same hygienic conditions that you have been accustomed to, you will maintain yourself at the increased weight on the increased supply of food.

Pygmies and Giants

Now, all this involves clearly enough a greatly increased rate of activity on the part of the bodily organs of assimilation and repair. It is a situation on all fours with that of the countryman whose rate of brain activity has been stimulated by an increased mental demand.

No man will maintain that better, more nourishing and more liberal food rations, transformed into increased bodily tissue, with a consequent greater weight and greater muscular strength, would result in a loss of vitality or the shortening of a man's life.

Transforming Inertness into Alertness

Pygmies cannot become giants physically or intellectually. But as the puny youth can by systematic exercise broaden his frame and develop his muscles into at least a semblance of the athlete, and can then through his healthier appetite and his faster rate of repair maintain himself without effort at the new standard; so can the mentally inert call forth their reserves of energy and maintain a higher standard of activity and fruitfulness.

Few men live on the plane of their highest efficiency. Few search the recesses of the well-springs of power. The lives of most of us are passed among the shallows of the mind without thought of the possibilities that lurk within the deeper pools.

How the Mind Accumulates Energy

This accumulation of potential subconscious reserve energy is a result of the evolution of man and the growing complexity of his life.

No man could, if he would, respond to all the impulses to muscular action aroused in him by sense-impressions. It would be still less possible for him to respond to every impulse to muscular action awakened from the past with the remembered thought with which it is associated.

Desire, interest, attention and the selective will must pick and choose among these multitudinous tendencies to action.

Here, then, is another fact that has immediate bearing upon your ability to carry out any ambition you may have. Your every action is the net result of selection among a number of impulses and inhibitory forces or tendencies.

The Threshold of Inhibition

As a general thing, consciousness is made up of a number of conflicting ideas, each with its associated feeling and its impulse to action. Just what you do in any particular case depends upon what mental picture is strongest, is most vivid in consciousness, and thus able to overcome all contrary tendencies.

As life becomes more and more complex, the number and variety of our sensory experiences increase correspondingly. And so it comes about, that we have untold millions of sensory experiences, carrying with them the impulses to muscular response, none of which, on account of the multiplicity of conflicting ideas, is ever allowed to find release and actually take form in muscular activity.

Hidden Strength

The consequence is that only an exceedingly small proportion of the mental energy that is developed within us is ever actually displayed. The rest is somehow and somewhere locked up behind the inhibitory threshold. It is stored away in sub-consciousness with the sensory experiences of the past with which it is associated.

Giving a Man Scope

Quoting Mr. Waldo P. Warren: "Much of the strength within men is hidden, awaiting an occasion to reveal it. The head of a department in a great manufacturing concern severed his connection with the firm, his work falling upon a young man of twenty-five years. The young man rose to the occasion, and in a very short time was conceded to be the stronger executive of the two. He had been with the concern for several years, and was regarded as a bright fellow, but his marked success was a surprise to all who knew him—even to himself.

"The fact is, the young man had that ability all the time and didn't know it; and his employers didn't know it. He might have been doing greater things all along if there had been the occasion to reveal his strength.

"Do you employers and superior officers in business realize how much of this hidden strength there is in your men? Perhaps a word from you, giving certain men more scope, would liberate that ability for the development of both your business and your men.

"Do you workers know your own strength? Are you working up to your capacity? Or are you accepting the limits which the circumstances place about you?"

Chapter III

THE INITIATIVE ENERGY OF SUCCESS

Sources of Persistence

In such instances as we have recounted, men have found that persistent effort along certain lines has had the effect of making presently available what would otherwise be simply unused storage batteries of reserve power. What was the source and inspiration for this persistent effort?

You will say that it was ambition or patriotism or some similar semi-emotional influence. And so it was. But what is ambition, what is patriotism, what is any desire but a picturing to the mind's eye of the things desired, an awakening of a mental image of the result to be attained, the reward that is to follow certain efforts? And these mental pictures coming into consciousness have brought with them their associated emotions and their associated impulses to muscular action, impulses appropriate to the picture and automatically tending to work its realization.

These impulses constitute the whole of man's achieving power. They are the Initiative Energy of all Success.

Importance of the Mental Setting

When you are afflicted with doubt and fear, timidity and lack of confidence, this means that your mental inhibitions are too numerous, too high or too strong. Remove them and access is had to the latent energy of accumulated and creative thought complexes. You will then become buoyant, cheerful, overflowing with enthusiasm, and ready for a fresh, definite, active part in life.

Ideas, then, when latent, may be considered as possessing an energizing influence.

The same idea does not necessarily have the same effect upon the same persons at different times. What its effect may be at any time or with any individual depends upon the make-up of the consciousness in which it finds itself.

Ideas All Men Respond to

The setting of consciousness may be entirely different upon the present appearance of the particular idea from what it was on the occasion when this same idea last appeared. Yesterday there may have been present no conflicting tendencies, and this particular idea may therefore have been allowed free and joyous expression. Today other thoughts may be in the ascendency so that we look upon the idea of yesterday with a feeling of revulsion.

The thought that aroused new energy in you yesterday may then sicken you at your task today. The thought that stirs the soul of a vigorous man may shock the sensibilities of a delicate woman.

How to Exalt the Personality

Yet there are some ideas to which all men in varying degrees seem alike to respond. How often in battle have the failing spirits of an army been revived by the appearance of the leader shouting his battle-cry and waving his shining sword! How often have men been roused to heights of heroic achievement by the strains of martial music! How often have troops spent with exhaustion responded to the call of such simple phrases as "The Flag," "Our Country," "Liberty," or such songs as "The Marseillaise," "God Save the King," "Dixie"! These phrases are but the signs of ideas, yet the sounding of these phrases has summoned these ideas into consciousness, and the summoning of these ideas into consciousness has placed undreamed-of and immeasurable foot-pounds of energy on the hair-trigger of action.

"Good Starters" and "Strong Finishers"

And so it is with you. Down deep in the inmost chambers of your soul are untouched stores of energy that properly applied will exalt your personality and illumine your career.

But to find and claim these hidden riches you must persevere. You must endure.

In a Marathon race it is endurance that wins. The graceful sprinter who is off with a leap at the bark of the pistol soon falls by the wayside.

Life is a Marathon in which persistence triumphs.

There are many "good starters," but few "strong finishers." That is why the failures so outnumber the successes.

Steps in Self-Development

The man who travels fastest does more than he is told to do. To merely comply with a fixed routine is to fall short of one's duty. The progressive man adds to the work of today his preparation for the work of tomorrow. He delights in attempting more and more difficult tasks, because in every task he sets himself he sees a step forward in the development of his own abilities. He loves his work more than he loves his pay, and he delves deeper than the exigencies of the moment require, because he craves the power to do more.

Most men start with enthusiasm. No hours are too long, no task too difficult. But soon they tire. And lacking will-power to persist, they succumb to the lure of distracting interests. They become disheartened and indifferent. And so they fail.

Saving a Thousand a Year

A young man married. He was proprietor of a flourishing "general" store in Princeton, Indiana. He and his bride forthwith resolved that they could and would lay aside out of their income a thousand dollars a year for ten years, by which time they would have ten thousand dollars and accumulated interest and could go into business in a big city. At the end of the first year, when they took stock of their savings, they decided that thereafter, instead of trying to save a thousand dollars a year for ten years, they would undertake to save ten dollars a year for a thousand years and would be more apt to succeed. Today they are just where they began.

You all know such men—men who are always starting and never finishing.

Looking for a "Soft Snap"

Ninety-five per cent of the men who go into business are "quitters." The very first disappointment sends them scurrying to cover. They begin to look for a "soft snap" away from the firing line. Is it any wonder that so few reach any great success?

That there is an enormous lack of appropriation of energy in most men's lives is an undoubted fact. Just where this energy is stored, and just what its eternal significance may be, is immaterial to our purpose.

It may be that this reserve is Nature's safeguard against our extravagance.

It may be, as some philosophers contend, that the subconscious, with its vast stores of energy, is a higher, more spiritual phase of man.

Drawing Power from on High

It may be that the subconscious is for each one of us his individual segment of the Divine Essence—that it marks our "at-one-ment" with God.

It may be that to evoke these latent energies is to call upon those resources of our being which are the embodiment within us of the spirit of the Creator of all things.

It may be that this Divine Essence, if adequately aroused, may exert an absolute transcendence over material things and lift humanity to a God-like plane.

"What we call man," wrote Emerson, "the eating, drinking, planting, counting man, does not, as we know him, represent himself, but mis-represents himself. Him we do not respect; but the real soul whose organ he is, would he let it appear through his action, would make our knees bend." "I said, ye are gods," quoth the Psalmist. "Be ye perfect, even as your Father," was the injunction of the Master.

Whatever the eternal significance of your latent energy may be, the fact remains that it is yours, and yours to use.

If you are to succeed, if you are to do big things, you must be a man of "doggedness." You must keep your eyes trained everlastingly upon the vision of the thing you want. You must stay in the race until you get your "second wind." You must be master of yourself and draw freely on your stored-up powers.

The Man Who Lasts

Do as we shall tell you in this Course and you will become a master man, the kind of man who "lasts," the kind of man who works his imagination overtime, the kind of man who can strain his energies to the utmost and then, finding himself still a failure, can rise "like the glow of the sun" to do bolder and bigger things— the kind of man who wins.

Chapter IV

HOW TO AVOID WASTES THAT DRAIN THE ENERGY OF SUCCESS

Speeding the Bullet Without Aiming

We have shown you that you have within you the potentialities of success in the form of latent mental energy. We have shown you that your ability to achieve depends upon your ability to utilize to the full your underground mental resources.

But success demands that you do more than merely use all your mental energies. You must use them intelligently.

Why Most Men Fail

Most men fail because they speed the bullet without aiming. They fire at random, and so bag no game.

Your pent-up mental energy is the powder in the cartridge. Its usefulness depends upon the man behind the gun.

To succeed in business you must intelligently control and direct (1) your own mental energies, (2) the mental energies of others.

The course of the average man through life is an aimless zigzag. It has neither direction nor purpose. It represents wasted energy capriciously expended.

Mental energy is like water: it has a tendency to scatter. It is diffusive. It seeks release in a thousand different directions at the same time.

As a boy, first learning to write, you were unable to prevent the simultaneous squirming of tongue and legs, all ludicrously irrelevant to your purpose of writing. So now, as a business man, unless you have learned the secret of self-mastery, you are unable to concentrate your efforts, your attention is easily distracted, you exhaust yourself in displays of passion, you are forever doing things during business hours that have no relation to your business, you are forever doing things in connection with your business that do not contribute to its progress, you expend just as much energy as the accomplished executive or the successful "hustler," but you fritter it away in unprofitable activities.

The Successful Promoter

To correct this is to gain mastery and power.

Concentrate your mental energies on one thing at a time. Stop spreading them around. The promoter may have a dozen big enterprises under way at once, but he takes them up one at a time. He transfers his whole mind and thought from one to the next. You cannot of course be eternally doing the same thing; but make no mistake about it, the only way to succeed at anything is to consciously control your mental energies. You may throw them now into this attack, now into another; but you must always have a tight grip on yourself, or you cannot succeed.

The Human Dynamo

You will often hear some "live-wire" business man spoken of as a "human dynamo." He has the faculty of turning out a stupendous amount of work in a comparatively short time. How he can carry in his mind the details of so many large projects, how he can accomplish so much in actual, tangible results in many directions, how he can pull the strings of so many enterprises without getting lost in the maze of detail, is the marvel of his associates. And yet this man is never "hurried, nor flurried, nor worried." But every word and every act is straight to the point and productive of results worthwhile.

Cool Brains and Hot Boxes

"A cool brain is the reverse of a hot box. It carries the business of the day along with a steady drive, and is invariably the mark of the big man. The man who dispatches his work quietly, promptly and efficiently, with no trace of fuss and flurry, is a big man. It is not the hurrying, clattering and chattering individual who turns off the most work. He may imagine he is getting over a lot of track, but he wastes far more than the necessary amount of steam in doing it. The fable of the hare and the tortoise would not be a bad primer for a number of us, and the lesson relearned would not only be beneficial in a business-producing way, but it would help us in the full enjoyment of our work."

Marvelous Increased Efficiency Handling "Pig"

Progress in mental efficiency must result from the application of knowledge of the mental machine. Just as we watch the steam-engine and the electric motor to see that they are not "overloaded," so we must watch the mental machine, that no more power be turned on than can be profitably employed.

This principle has already been applied to physical labor by Mr. Frederick W. Taylor in his ground-breaking studies in "scientific management." Mr. Taylor's celebrated experiments in the handling of pig-iron, by which the quantity handled in a day by one man was increased from twelve and one-half tons to forty-seven and one-half tons, "showed that a man engaged in such extremely heavy work could only be under load forty-three per cent of the working day, and must be entirely free from load for fifty-seven per cent, to attain the maximum efficiency."

"Overloaded" Human Engines

There is no reason why efficiency in mental effort should not be gauged just as accurately as in muscular activity. If there are times when your wits are not as keen, when you have not the same grasp of fundamentals, as at other times, it is because you are mentally "overloaded." It may be the result of a great variety of causes. It may be from too many hours of continuous mental effort. But the probabilities are that it is the result of vexation, worry, dissipation, or allowing the mind to be burdened with the strain of vicious, or at least irrelevant and distracting, impulses and desires. And so efficiency is lost.

Scientific Management of Self

The "human dynamo" is a man who long ago learned the lesson of scientific management of his own mental forces. He does one thing at a time, and does it the best he knows how. He directs the whole power of his mentality to the one problem and solves it with accuracy and dispatch. There is no more of a "load" on his "gray matter" than there is on that of the fretting, fuming, finger-biting fritterer, but every pound of steam is spent in useful work.

Look at the victim of St. Vitus' dance. There you have an illustration of wasted energy. And it is mental energy, for every muscular movement represents the release of thought power. The mental lives of most men are equally aimless. They are lives of ceaseless activity producing nothing.

Psychological Causes of Waste

Sometimes it happens that a man is not working to advantage because of some defect in his physical make-up. He may have defective vision or some peculiarity of hearing that renders him unable to respond as quickly as he should to the demands made upon him. If these defects are ascertained, it is usually a simple matter to correct the defects by mechanical means or readjust the relative duties of different persons so that the defects will be minimized.

Tests for Sensory Defects

Where large numbers of people are employed, it is comparatively easy to use tests for discovering defects of sight or hearing by simple apparatus without requiring the services of a high-priced expert. By adopting these test methods any manager of a large industrial establishment can satisfy himself whether his employees are up to certain normal standards. He can even apply the tests to himself.

Optical tests can be conducted by securing an ordinary letter chart such as is used by oculists and opticians. Seat the subject twenty feet away. If he can read all the lines of letters from the largest down to the smallest his eyesight is practically perfect. In a large percentage of cases the smaller lines of type are blurred and invisible. To detect the cause and degree of defects of the eyes it is necessary to try out the eyes by using a trial spectacle frame and inserting detached lenses before the right eye and the left eye alternately. One of the most common forms of defective vision is astigmatism. A chart has been designed with a series of circles and straight lines radiating from the center. If the subject is astigmatic he will see some of the straight lines distinctly while others will be blurred. For instance, one or two of the vertical lines may appear very black and strong while all others will look like a hazy network. This defect, due to unevenness of the spherical surface of the eyeball, is easily corrected with properly ground glasses.

Defects in hearing can be easily determined by means of an "acoumeter." This little instrument measures the acuteness of the hearing very accurately by means of shot dropped from varying heights upon strips of glass, copper and cardboard. Tests with this device indicate whether the subject's hearing is above or below normal.

Mental Friction and Inner Whirlwinds

Stop wasting your energy.

Heretofore you have used your powers in a more or less haphazard way, with a vast amount of waste and no efficient direction. From now on you are to exercise more intelligence in this respect and make all your energies contribute to your business progress and your personal success.

You are losing power in fruitless outward activities.

You are losing power in the thinking of useless thoughts. You cannot stop the ceaseless activity of the mind. But you can conserve its forces by directing them into channels that are worthwhile.

You are losing power in a turmoil of inward mental strains and in-harmonies. Catch yourself at some moment when you are forging ahead in a crowded day's work. You will then see what an inner whirlwind of excitement is in progress, what stresses and strains are at work, what contrary impulses, what frictions and obstacles are being overcome.

Now, to the engineer every one of these words—

friction, obstacle, strain—spells loss of efficiency, and in this Course we shall teach you how you may do away with antagonistic impulses, may bring your combined mental forces to bear upon the common enemy, and may hurl yourself into the struggles of business and practical life with a joyful and headlong impetuosity that no obstacle can withstand.

Prominent Traits of Great Achievers

Professor Walter Dill Scott, of Northwestern University, has said: "In studying the lives of contemporary business men, two facts stand out pre-eminently. The first is that their labors have brought about results that to most of us would have seemed impossible. Such men appear as giants in comparison with whom ordinary men sink to the size of pygmies. The second fact, which a study of successful business men (or any class of successful men) reveals, is that they never seem rushed for time.

"Such men have time to devote to objects in no way connected with their business. It cannot be regarded as accidental that this characteristic of mind is found so commonly among successful men during the years of their most fruitful labor. According to the American ideal, the man who is sure to succeed is the one who is continuously 'keyed up to concert pitch'—who is ever alert and is always giving attention to his business or profession."

And again: "It is not necessarily true that the greatest and most constant display of energy accompanies the greatest presence of energy. The tug-boat on the river is constantly blowing off steam and making a tremendous display of energy, while the ocean liner proceeds on its way without noise and without commotion. The man who frets and fumes, who is nervous and excited, is strung up to such a pitch that energy is being dissipated in all directions."

Many business men know they are going at a pace that kills, and at the same time they feel that they are accomplishing too little. For such the pertinent question is, How may I reduce the expenditure of energy without reducing the efficiency of my labor?

One of the busiest and most efficient men in England is quoted as having explained his own accomplishment of big results with the least expenditure of effort: "By organizing myself to run smoothly, as well as my business; by schooling myself to keep cool, and to do what I have to do without expending more nervous energy on the task than is necessary; by avoiding all needless friction. In consequence, when I finish my day's work, I feel nearly as fresh as when I started."

Why a Man Breaks Down

The late Professor James, of Harvard University, often referred to as the founder of modern psychology, spoke thus disparagingly of untrained effort: "Your convulsive worker breaks down and has bad moods so often that you never know where he may be when you most need his help,—he may be having one of his 'bad days.' We say that so many of our fellow-countrymen collapse and have to be sent abroad to rest their nerves, because they work so hard. I suspect that this is an immense mistake, I suspect that neither the nature nor the amount of our work is accountable for the frequency and the severity of our breakdowns, but that their cause lies rather in those absurd feelings of hurry and having no time, in the breathlessness and tension, that anxiety of feature and solicitude for results, that lack of inner harmony and ease, in short, by which with us the work is apt to be accompanied."

How to Economize Effort

The fact is that to be a truly busy man you must be never in a hurry. You must work systematically. You must economize effort. You must permit no distractions and do your work leisurely. You must take time to think things over in a natural way. You must waste no thoughts in business hours on social or pleasurable pursuits that would dissipate your mental capital. You must work when you work, and you may play when you play, but your business must be the most fascinating of games and the only one you play during business hours.

How Your Mental Capital is Dissipated

Another thing you need is poise. One trouble with you now is that you waste your priceless powers in useless anxiety.

The minute business falls off you begin to worry. You fritter your mental energies in fretting until you are incapable of real thought, and being unable to think your way out you get excited.

Remember it is all just a game, and you are in it only for the fun of the thing. You will never win out if you persist in tearing your hair.

Before he crossed the Rubicon Julius Cesar was staggered at the greatness of the undertaking before him. The more he reflected and took counsel of his friends, the greater loomed the difficulties of the attempt and the more appalling the calamities his passage of that river would bring upon the Roman world. But when at last with the cry, "The die is cast!" he plunged into the river, there was an end for him to mental dissension, a freedom to plan and execute, an expansion of courage and power.

Conquering Indecision

So it will be with you. With doubt and uncertainty the pressure may be high in the gauge,
but the engine does not move. Make up your
mind, and you release energies previously
wasted in conflicts between opposing thought
complexes struggling for supremacy.

Why "Christian Science" Works

A fine illustration of this is shown in the religious experience known as conversion. To the convert, conversion means the profound acceptance of a mighty spiritual truth. It means positive knowledge taking the place of doubt or indifference. Conflicting ideas are no longer present in his consciousness. Pent-up energies are released. He wants to do things. His soul is fired with overmastering impulses to action. He wants to go forth and preach the gospel of his faith. He is lifted to a high plane of exhilaration. He experiences the "peace that passed understanding."

"Christian Science," "Truth," "The New Thought," and similar movements all achieve their really marvelous results in much the same way. All proclaim doctrines of exuberant optimism, having a tendency to banish fear-thoughts and self-consciousness and self-depreciation, and to set up in their stead ideas of courage and of achievement and of individual power. If these teachings are successful—that is to say, if they inherently possess the right appeal for the particular individual—they have the happy effect of begetting a stoical indifference to petty physical disorders and social vexations and bringing about a concentration upon the main business of life of the mental energies thus previously wasted.

How to Release Pent-Up Power

Decide the matter that is troubling you. Make an end of hesitation and uncertainty and fear. Your very act of decision will release large stores of pent-up mental power and add immeasurably to your effectiveness.

So long as you are in doubt and perplexity conflicting ideas and impulses balance each other. You are not then a man of action; you are a wavering coward. You are afflicted with paralysis of will and mental stagnation.

Decide the matter—that is to say, let one mental picture assume a greater vividness than the other until it possesses your soul—and forthwith the banked fires of your mental energy will burst into flame.

Another thing: Stop wasting your time.

How much time do you spend in rest and relaxation? How much should you spend? Can you answer these questions accurately?

Proper Ratio Between Work and Rest

Thomas A. Edison has contended for years that four hours' sleep a day was sufficient for any man. He has conducted experiments with a large number of men, giving careful attention to matters of diet and exercise, and the results have seemed in a measure to support his theory.

Dr. Fred W. Eastman reports that owing to pressure of work he was recently unable to get more than three or four hours' sleep out of the twenty-four during a period of many months, and that so far from being hurt by it he gained five pounds. He says: "If restoration during sleep is a task so relatively small, the question arises whether, in order to complete restoration, it is necessary for us to spend so much time in sleep as we do. Perhaps on account of popular opinion and personal habit, we waste much time in this jelly-fish condition that could more profitably be spent in active pursuit of our ambitions. The answer, of course, depends upon the nature of our occupations. If there is muscular effort involved, with a correspondingly large amount of waste in the cells and blood, eight hours or more are probably necessary. But if the work is of a sedentary nature, and mainly of the brain, there is naturally a smaller quantity of accumulated waste, and less time is required for removal.

Many are the instances of great men, past and present, who have lived healthily and worked unceasingly and strenuously on only four or five hours of sleep, or half the laborer's portion. Surely we do not suppose that these men were or are physically different from others, but rather that by inclination or necessity they have developed a habit of sleeping intensely for a short period, with resulting gain of time and efficiency."

Determining Your Norm of Efficiency

So far as this matter of relaxation, rest and sleep is concerned, the rule to follow is obviously this: Determine accurately by experiment the proper relation between periods of work and periods of rest in your own case, then increase your efficiency by maintaining this relation.

In Denmark they feed cows scientifically. Day by day they increase the allowance of milk-producing food. Day by day the yield of milk increases. At last there comes a day when measurement shows that there is no longer any increase in the production of milk. They then decrease the food till the output of milk diminishes. So they determine the normal.

So with you and your hours of work and leisure. Give more and more time to your business each day until there comes an impairment in the quality of your work. Stop short of this. You have found your norm of efficiency.

Chapter V

THE SECRET OF MENTAL EFFICIENCY

Where Energy Is Stored

You are called upon to master and conserve the innate energies of your mind. This means that you must (1) find out where these energies are stored, and (2) learn the conditions that determine their activity.

All past experiences are conserved within us in the form of complexes. These complexes consist of ideas, emotions and impulses to muscular activity. By the primary law of association the recall to consciousness of any one of these component elements of a complex brings with it all the rest.

Bodily Effects of Ideas

For example, the ideas pertaining to any terrifying experience, when recalled to consciousness, bring with them the trembling, the wildly beating heart, the shaking knees, with which they were originally accompanied. The victim of stage-fright feels his knees give way and that he is sinking to the floor; his heart beats tumultuously, cold perspiration covers his body, he blushes, his mouth is dry, and his voice sticks in his throat. Afterwards, alone in his own room, the memory of that dreadful moment, the thought of another appearance before that audience, will be accompanied by the same physiological effects.

Impulses and Inhibitions

Every such bodily movement is an expression of energy. The recall to consciousness of the terrifying experience, the recall of the picture of the assembled audience, these things automatically produce bodily activities. So we must conclude that Every idea in memory has associated with it the potential energy necessary for the production of muscular movement.

It does not necessarily follow that the recall to consciousness of a given idea will be invariably followed by an outwardly visible muscular activity expressive of its energy. Just as the mere presence of an idea in consciousness tends to bring about a movement, so the presence of a contrary idea will tend to inhibit it.

Try to imagine that you are bending your forefinger. At the same time hold it straight. Your finger will actually tremble with the dammed-up energy of the repressed impulse. But the finger will not actually move, because the idea of its not moving is just as much a part of your consciousness as the idea of its moving. Put out of your consciousness this thought of the finger's not moving, and forthwith the finger will bend.

Your conduct during your waking hours is thus always the result of opposing forces, some tending in one direction, others tending to counteract the first. Thus there comes about a great waste of mental power and an appalling loss of individual efficiency.

Training for Mental "Team-Work"

In the language of sport, you are suffering from a lack of mental "team work." The effect is the same as if the members of a football team, instead of combining their forces against the opposing side, should spend their time in restraining one another.

It requires but one step, and not a difficult one at that, to lead you to the conclusion that the solution of this problem lies in having in consciousness at any one moment only such ideas as harmonize. Let that condition prevail, and the potential energies of all ideas in consciousness must flow together in a broad stream of useful and exhilarating activity.

Rust and the "Daily Grind"

Your work should be a source of pleasure to you. If it is simply a disagreeable task that has to be performed, if it is a "daily grind," if you have to hold yourself to it by unremitting effort of the will, you are no better than a rusty engine, and all your workings will be accompanied by jars, frictions, and complaining squeaks that bespeak a positively wicked loss of power.

Hold the right thoughts persistently in mind, and you cannot help working steadily on toward the goal you are thinking of. Keep steadily at work with the right thoughts persistently in mind and success is sure to come.

Success, then, lies in the concentration of mental energies. And this concentration is to be brought about by holding in consciousness only those ideas that harmonize.

Ideas That Harmonize

There must be the greatest discrimination and care used in the selection of these ideas that are to constitute such a co-ordinating consciousness. There must be a "re-imaging" or imagination in a literal and practical sense of those ideas only that carry with them impulses to motion in the same general direction. You must have a set purpose in life, and you must yield your powers without hindrance and without reservation to the accomplishment of that set purpose.

Five Rules for Conserving Energy

I. You must exercise deliberate, patient and persistent watchfulness to detect and repress all useless bodily movements. You have all sorts of silly habits, twitchings, jerkings, itchings, winkings, shrugs, frowns, coughs, snifflings and odd and meaningless gestures. Watch yourself. Do these things no more. Save your eyes and ears and hands and nerves, all your mental energy, for useful effort.

II. You must give yourself, mind and body, to one thing at a time, disregarding all that would lure you from your chosen task.

III. You must acquire a self-conscious sense of your own self-mastery. It will help you to acquire this feeling if you will continually assert, "I can and will accomplish anything that I am determined upon! I have the power of will! I will accomplish this thing! I will!" Make these assertions with all the force and intensity of your whole being until you are pervaded with a sense of your own power. Do this faithfully, and in time this courageous and manly attitude will become an inherent part of your personality.

IV. You must have confidence. And when we say confidence we do not mean a purely intellectual conviction. We mean a profoundly emotional faith. It will help you to cultivate this feeling of confidence if you will affirm many times a day, "I have implicit confidence in myself! I have perfect faith in my own powers! I am absolute master of myself and of my career!" Practice affirmations of this kind persistently, and in time your mind will have permanently acquired the habit of facing the facts of life in the way essential to success.

V. You must exert a favorable influence upon the mental attitude of those about you. This is not so difficult as it would appear. You cannot yourself acquire will-power, confidence and courage without impressing others with your possession of these qualities. Personalities are revealed one to another by faint and suggestive activities all unconsciously perceived. Your concentration of energy will inspire others. You will radiate an "atmosphere" of success. You will subtly influence your associates. You will be a force to reckon with, and the world will know it. Your air of success will draw others to you, will bring business and goodwill, and men and money will seek a share in your enterprises.

Master your mental energies, train them, concentrate them,—thus only may you win riches with honor.

Thus broadly put, there is, or perhaps it would be more accurate to say there seems to be, nothing startlingly new about this proposition.

The world has always realized that singleness of purpose, concentration of effort, is essential to success.

But in the past the world has possessed no formula by which these qualities might be acquired.

Men have endeavored to create in themselves the necessary qualities for success, having no knowledge of the mental elements that went into their composition.

They have tried to run the mental engine knowing nothing of its mechanism.

Business Luck and "Blue-Sky" Theories

Some few have been lucky, but the path has been strewn with a thousand failures to one that passed on to success.

There are some business men who look upon psychology as "blue-sky" theorizing or "new thought." There are others who have a hazy idea that it is a sort of unfathomable mystery intended to amuse long-haired scientists. The truth is that every one of these same business men, if he is getting ahead, is unconsciously using psychological principles to the profit of his own business every day in the year.

Devices for Commercial Efficiency

In the books that are to follow we shall show you the immense practical value of a truly scientific psychology. You shall come into the psychological laboratory with us and work out rational, scientific and exact methods by which, without possibility of failure and with but reasonable effort, you can at any moment completely concentrate your mental powers. You shall be instructed in simple devices for mastering scattered energies, repressing wasteful habits, banishing depressive moods and raising yourself to a far higher level of commercial efficiency.

Applied Psychology

Volume 1: Psychology and Achievement

Volume 2: Making your own World

Volume 3: Driving Power of Thought

Volume 4: The Trained Memory

Volume 5: Power of Mental Imagery

Volume 6: Psychic Energy

Volume 7: Processes and Personality

Volume 8: Mind Mechanism

Volume 9: Mind Mastery

Volume 10: Technique of Success

Volume 11: External Efficiency Factors

Volume 12: Specific Applications

www.ingramcontent.com/pod-product-compliance
Lightning Source LLC
Chambersburg PA
CBHW051345170526
45166CB00002B/968